BIGGIE

CAUSE SIZE MATTERS

BY S. E. MCKENZIE

DEDICATION
To everyone who has been left out in the cold

THIS BOOK IS A BOOK OF SPECULATIVE FICTION
Characters, companies, governments, places, events, are either products of the author's imagination or used fictitiously. Any resemblance to persons (living or dead), companies, governments, places and/or events, is a coincidence and unintentional.

TABLE OF CONTENTS

BIGGIE

BIGGIE

I

Time
A circle
The beginning

And the ending; everlasting;
When seen from the sky
By those not yet sleeping inside infinity;

No longer able to touch
Or be touched
The way mere mortals can be.

Vibrating
Pulsating
Now so free.

What we see
Depends
On transparency.

II

She looks into the mirror
She does it everyday
She looks into the mirror

BIGGIE

Cause she was brought up that way.

She sees the reflection
Of herself
In her projection

Of you.
In a world broken in two
By the sad man

Whose heart yearns to be free

From his reflection;
Free from his projection;
Free from his suggestion;

While time ravaged our youth.

Vibrating
Pulsating
Not yet free

Not yet floating inside Infinity.

III
Inaccurate missile;
Small warhead;
Randomness;

Created our luck by chance;
We ducked Demented Society's savagery;
While Nouveau Gestapo stared;

Did not care;
About our vulnerability
Even though big guns were all around.

No Time to dance
Or linger in our youth
We were faced with a terrible truth.

We were not allowed in the polling booth

For Inequity was all around;
We treaded lightly
On hillbilly ground.

Our lives may be shortened
By Big Guns Projections;
Or worse yet, weapons of war

May turn us into something grotesque;
One day.
We will fade away anyway;

BIGGIE

From all of this.

But today we crave Universal Love
And refused
To be demoralized

By the Nouveau Gestapo's Tune.

In a world where the Regulator
Forced our silence;
He relished in his highness.

We could not protest;
Or suggest
A better way.

For the Regulator had the only say.
And the single explanation
To everything.

There was no dictator in the sky.
Time's boundaries
Were sucked away

Inside a black hole
No beginning or end
In a timeless soul

Of Infinity;
What one can see
Depends on Transparency.

We walk down the road
Of time
As age aged us savagely.

Love was under attack.
We seldom tired as we watched Love's back
We wanted the best; needed little rest.

We were the lost Generation
Or so the demented rulers said.
We responded to positive sensation

But we were hated instead.
The Regulator
Was like a vacuum

And many could not grow
Into tomorrow
For the barriers were too many;

BIGGIE

We saw the boundaries
Which shrunk our earth
And diminished what could have been

Self-worth.

A beautiful land of great hope
Free from Gestapo's rope;
The Regulator's command.

Created demand
In the only growth industry left
Social disorder.

Weakened by pain;
Empowered by Universal Love;
We knew what we needed

But there was never enough.
The demented lived in fear
Of everything they did not know

Or could not remember;
They said we did not belong
And made it so;

Yes, we were not a member

Of the Old Boy's Club
Some members could not remember;
Some carried the weapons which oppress;

People change when under duress;
So afraid to be dispossessed;
For we were still young.

As Youth; we were pushed away;
By the demented;
Empty heads already rented.

The future was promoted
In a state of hypocrisy
Watchers watched but could not see

In this land of mediocracy.
Ghetto Queen touched up her hair
Until it was golden

Put on her fancy underwear
And stared through people
As if they weren't there;

BIGGIE

She laughed as they spoke
So no one ever did;
Whenever they saw her coming

They hid.

To question the big guns
Was a form
Of Heresy; Just like

Questioning Demented Society's savagery.

The demented watchers were too blind to see
The entrance to the path
Which led to a great life

Was blocked by rusty barb wire
And holy gun-fire; so proud were they
When they fondled their Big Guns.

IV
Regulator had immunity;
Compulsive violator of humanity
In his quest to become a god;

Regulator turned back time
As the world grew smaller
And more bitter.

No constitution
In the land was higher
Than the Regulator's command.

V

The Regulator still ruled; still fooled;
The pigs on the mechanical farm.
The one with the biggest gun

Made everyone else run.
It was a crusade;
Big Guns were on parade.

I too had to run from his Killer Gun;
I ran into a foreign land
I hid my face, thought of a place

I once called home; still unknown to the living;
Where hearts could pulsate
Free; without feeling hate

Or worrying about the future state of Fate.

BIGGIE

Timeless and forever changing
Love might live forever
In a place called infinity Plus One.

We were the brave and had no gun;
We all refused to be slaves
To our fear; even though fear was always near.

And fear of others
Separated sisters and brothers;
We were still young enough

To call strangers our neighbors.

Ghetto Queen of mean
Pushed around people
Who were unseen.

"We don't want you here,
Dear";
She would sneer.

We knew she was dehumanized too;
For we could see the lie
In every tear that she could not cry.

The barriers were installed;
Made us hungry
Some ate out of garbage bins;

While the Regulator
Locked food away to rot
As Time's touch was gentler to some;

As the ones so fancy
Called us names;
They still were free

To play games;
While we spent
Some of the day

Finding a place to pee.

VI
Our Links in the food chain
Were broken
Our pain had awoken

Ghetto Queen
And the King of Bling
Looked away

BIGGIE

Gave up on today;
The turning point into tomorrow
Would now fade away.

Even though the Regulator
Tried to make it not so;
Time continued to touch

Everything and everyone.
Some were born
And some died;

Many lied
And others cried;
While the Regulator denied

That this was so.

Stability
A connection
A chance to be part of the selection

Was now out of reach
For inter-generational
Economic Warfare

Toxic and unfair;
So chaotic when so few
Dare to care;

Marginalization and alienation
Were greater than ever before.
And the Regulator

Said it wasn't so.

VII

The Watchers watched but could not see;
Had very little to say to us;
But we knew Time was on our side.

The builder of big
Had a new gig;
Just moments before the fall.

Reincarnated dinosaur
Wanted it all
To satisfy

His appetite;
So many had to die
Without a tear to cry;

BIGGIE

Without fear they uttered the lie;
We knew the truth
Despite our youth

For Natural law
Was round; a cycle;
Not a flat line;

Kept turning around;
Sometimes frozen in Time;
As smoke and ash blocked the sun;

Then their system crashed;
The old food-chain politics
Was now disrupted for evermore

For the store owner had locked the door.

And Time was on our side
Though the Regulator
Said it was not so.

For the smallest survived climate change before;
When the known world was turned upside down
The advantaged became the disadvantaged.

And the ceiling
Turned into a floor
The greatest roar roared no more.

As the biggest of all toppled;
And could not sustain
The appetite which caused so much fright.

The old dinosaur tried
All day and all night;
And us;

We avoided Society's Savagery

We had nothing to cling on to
So we were free
To walk into the unknown.

VIII

Ghetto Queen
Framed Mary Anne
Into something she was not

Gave Ghetto Queen
A feeling that she was still hot
While the King of Bling

BIGGIE

Promised her everything
That money could buy
No reason to make Mary-Anne cry.

"Accept the hate
That changes Fate and social standing,"
Ghetto Queen said

"Consider yourself fired.
We just stick with who we know
The way our Carrot Stick God

Tells us to,"
The Ghetto Queen said.
And the man who owned

Castles to rent and buy;
Sold hate
To the highest bidder

Empty space in his head for rent;
So demented
He did not care

When he made so many cry.
They all said their excitement
Was driven by their carrot stick god's energy

More intoxicating than the wine
That was made with the blood
Of the enemy who died covered in mud.

Shaped their frame of mind;
Made many unkind;
The Watchers could not see

For they were willfully blind.

IX

And we had Love's back;
So she could hold us
When we were under attack;

Our very selves
Were denied validation
We became the children

BIGGIE

Of the Lost Generation;
We grew trapped in alienation;
Always looking for something

To give us

A better sensation;
While Nouveau Gestapo
Was throwing around dope

Gestapo's rope in the War Economy;
We stood by Love's back;
Holding on to the hope

Only Love was able to give.

While Ghetto Queen
Listened to
The King of Bling

Who prayed for her Psyche-soul;

So Ghetto Queen could die in peace;
After living life at war;
She believed the King of Bling's promise

That her soul would live for evermore;
Lost within
Her steely four chambered heart;

She yelled at us
Whenever she saw us
Sometimes she complained to a watcher

Who looked but could not see

Culture of obstruction
And destruction
Was everywhere

And we tried to block it out
For Love's sake
We had her back.

While the barriers all around;
Cut us from any food supply;
We were starving to death;

We knew we were close
To our last breath
As we held on to Love a little too tight;

BIGGIE

All through the night;
We saw the light;
Shining onto our path;

And different directions
Led to different ways;
And different lives

At a Crossroad;
And I felt like a moving dot
On a scatter plot

Just a target to be shot.

And I took the path
Which led to the unknown
For I had nothing left to lose.

For Diversity was just the Regulator's word
Patronizing, stigmatizing, dividing;
Just double talk behind the sneer

Projecting fear;
Watchers always near;
Always watching but could not see

Their own hypocrisy.

Manufactured a skid row;
The Regulator divided a whole city;
Did not care about our sorrow;

In the prison style city;
Bulldozing what was not pretty;
Creating negative situations

With unfair accusations.
And we never had a chance
To increase our social standing there.

As they closed down the schools
The ones who stayed grew into fools;
Stuck in the prison city;

The Nouveau Gestapo
Stared at us
With steely eyes

BIGGIE

That marginalized;
For the Regulator
His highness; contrasted

With our lowness;
Time around us
Froze into slowness.

The Final Hour
Turned our world upside down
While our progress moved backwards.

The Watchers watched
But could not see
As we tried to save our

The Watchers watched us
While some grew demoralized;
Lost their self-esteem;

Could not put together
Their broken dream
For the Regulator

Manufactured Skid Row.
Nowhere left to grow
Without sorrow.

The Watchers watched
Standing under the sign
Which buzzed out the word diversity.

The Watchers watched
Fate go by without a tear in their eyd;
Easier to hate than to innovate;

The boundary of our growth
Stopped at every barrier
Which was said to beautify

Though we knew the lie

Fences were all around
To keep the nature in
Which was dying and could not thrive;

For Nature too was not allowed to be free.

THE END

Produced by S.E. McKenzie Productions
First Print Edition June 2015

Enquiries: 1(778)992-2453
Mailing Address:
S. E. McKenzie Productions
168 B 5th St.
Courtenay, BC
V9N 1J4

Email Address:
messidartha@aol.com

http://www.amazon.com/SarahMcKenzie/e/B00H9RWX48/

www.ingramcontent.com/pod-product-compliance
Lightning Source LLC
Chambersburg PA
CBHW060548030426
42337CB00021B/4486